Conversation Skills For Beginners:

Effective Communication Strategies to Improve Your Social Skills and Being Able to Talk and Connect with Anyone

By

Dale Blake

Table of Contents

Introduction 5

Chapter 1. The Basics 6

Chapter 2. Categories of Communication 9

    1. Verbal and Nonverbal 10

    2. Oral and Written 12

    3. Formal and informal 14

Chapter 3. Keys to an Effective Communication 16

Final Words 28

Thank You Page 30

Conversation Skills For Beginners: Effective Communication Strategies to Improve Your Social Skills and Being Able to Talk and Connect with Anyone

By Dale Blake

© Copyright 2014 Dale Blake

Reproduction or translation of any part of this work beyond that permitted by section 107 or 108 of the 1976 United States Copyright Act without permission of the copyright owner is unlawful. Requests for permission or further information should be addressed to the author.

This publication is designed to provide accurate and authoritative information in regard to the subject matter covered. This work is sold with the understanding that the publisher is not engaged in rendering legal, accounting, or other professional services. If legal advice or other expert assistance is required, the services of a competent professional person should be sought.

First Published, 2014

Printed in the United States of America

Introduction

The world is an enormous system of different kinds of matter that exchange information. Such act is known as communication, which range from molecular levels to organizations and governments, from human beings to creatures living in bodies of water. Things communicate sometimes without being aware of doing so, just like you sometimes catch yourself off-guard, speaking to yourself in front of the mirror – you call it 'talking out loud'. Although every creature of this earth does communicate with others, human beings have a higher level of dealing with their kind, as it involves exchange of not only information, but also emotions, spirituality and others. As the person in you has the human nature to desire to improve itself in effectively communicating, as in anything, it is important for you to understand the craft first and foremost.

Chapter 1. The Basics

Communication is lexically defined as the act of using words, sounds, signs, or behavior to express ideas, thoughts, and feelings to someone else. To communicate means to send information to a receiver. Basically, to communicate is to convey. There are actually too many ways to define, complicate or simplify the essence of communication, that several theories have emerged to attempt on explaining them as thoroughly as they could be explained, but one claim states that no single specific field of study can be identified as a communication theory, despite the 'growing profusion of theories' about it. Models of communication, however, endeavor to explain the communication process. Some common ones are the constructionist, the interactive and the transactional.

A simple and timeless scheme is called the linear communication model, which presents the basic concept of communication being the process of sending and receiving messages, shows the transferring of 'source' from the sender to the receiver. It is illustrated showing four boxes aligned horizontally, with the words, source, receiver, source and receiver, respectively, with arrows in between, directed to each box on the right.

Another model of communication, popularized as Berlo's, on the other hand, shows that there are subcomponents under its very basic elements, which are the sender, the message, the channel, and the receiver. Although many other models and theories claim addition to these essential components of communication, this model maintains the four, and elaborates each through the elements under each. The sender, or the person responsible for creating a message, is shown to be affected by five things: communication skills, attitude, knowledge, social system and culture. The message, as indicated, is not limited to content, as it is only one portion of it. It further includes its elements, treatment, structure and what is called as codes. The third part, which is the channel, employs the four of the five senses, except olfaction: hearing or audition, seeing or sight, touching or tactility, tasting or gustation. It also includes feeling, or emotion. It is worth noting that the components under the receiver, or the person receiving the created message, are exactly the same as the sender, and this shows how the cycle of communication may work, as the receiver of the message may eventually act as the sender of the same, or something else, for that matter. The communication process, nonetheless is deemed complete once the receiver understands the sender's message.

Chapter 2. Categories of Communication

The different paradigms formulated by experts on communication have been designed to fit in any type of communication, be it verbal or nonverbal, oral or written, formal or informal, simple or complicated. In order to be excellent in communication, it is essential that you realize the significance of non-verbal communication in its entirety, and how it affects the message you are trying to convey verbally. It is also proper to know when some communications are best written or spoken, and how to be most appropriate with the tone that you use in delivering the information. For communication to become effective, it is necessary that the desired effect becomes the actual result of the encounter. It is of great significance that your conversing with another person allows you to make him or her understand what you really mean to say.

1. Verbal and Nonverbal

Verbal communication is basically also known as spoken or oral. Literally, the term, 'verbal' relates to, or consists of words. More radically, it is defined as 'consisting of or using of words only and not involving action'. Therefore, considering the latter definition, verbal communication is the type which is limited to the very words used in delivering a message. It does not include intonation, gestures, facial expressions, eye movements, or anything that are not words. Using such definition, verbal communication, although known as oral communication, can be seen clearly in media such as plain text messaging, letter writing, the use of telegraph in the recent times, and in the even earlier times, the use of the Morse code. In such examples, considering that emoticons and differences in handwriting are available, there are no other elements but the words themselves. One may say the message is clean, while another may say the lack of emotions in the message may be much more prone to misinterpretation.

As they say, only less than 20 per cent of what you say comes from words. This means that more than 80 per cent are nonverbal cues. These signals are those other things involving communication, other than words. They range from a blink, posture, tone of voice, pitch, proximity or distance, touch, eye contact, and so many other things. This also contains the emotions you incorporate in the conversation, both intentionally and unintentionally. Nonverbal communication is what it means when somebody tells you that what you are saying is far different from what you are saying. Saying 'go' may mean 'I encourage you to go after your dreams', while the very same word may also mean 'don't'. They are one and the same word, yet the major difference lies on how you say it. Indeed, it's how you say it.

2. Oral and Written

In simple terms, oral means 'of or relating to the mouth'. You may hear 'oral' when distinguishing your medications from that which you take by applying, by inhaling or through injections. You swallow your oral meds, as you do so by your mouth. Oral also means spoken, rather than written.

Oral communication therefore is interacting by speaking. While it refers primarily to spoken verbal communication, it cannot be detached from the use of written (or illustrated) materials and non-verbal elements. These, as explained earlier are necessary in making your message clearer, and much easier to be understood by your target receiver. Speaking for some is easier than writing, as it is more spontaneous, and gives an opportunity to clarify. It is less particular with rules, and allows you to employ as much nonverbal elements as you wish to. On the other hand, others prefer writing as a means of communication, as it apparently frees them of the need for spontaneity, and allows them to correct mistakes without the receiver witnessing it.

Written communication obviously did not start being how it is at present. Its history traces back to the time people used pictograms made of stone. It eventually became progressed when paper, papyrus, clay and other similar materials became available, which paved the way for the portability of written communication. The third major phase of the present history of this type of communication is what you have now, which was made possible by the advent of the use of electronic signals, allowing you to receive messages on your phone, on your laptop, or on your bigger computer unit.

Much of what is communicated through 'writing' are words, especially during the second phase of the mentioned history, but there are also ways to incorporate emotions through written interactions. In paper, one's handwriting may vary, conveying the supposed lacking nonverbal elements, while emoticons and stickers have been made available to express similar expressions to further make clear the information you would like to transfer during your chatting and texting activities.

3. Formal and informal

The differences in the extent of formality in communication are usually discussed in organizational atmospheres. This usually depends on the type of your workplace, and what kind of interaction is deemed most effective by your company. The most basic principle here is that companies need to be able to communicate effectively – both within it and outside.

Formal communication is usually used in conveying information among units of an organization, both vertically and horizontally. The former means that information is transferred between decision makers and implementers, following an organizational hierarchy, while the latter involves interaction between and among same-level officers or employees.

In a formal setting, you need to align your communications with existing rules and conventions of business etiquette. As such, accountability is essential, taking into consideration functionality in meetings, conferences, letters, announcements, and even telephone conversations. It is most important to recognize and keep in mind the consequences of your actions in communicating information in the formal setting.

This does not strictly say though, that all organizational communication is entirely formal. When you deal with your colleagues outside of the formal arena of your workplace, you may go spontaneous and casual. Informal communication may be viewed as social, the way you may connect with friends or acquaintances. This way of communicating is seen in grapevines, chitchats, or small talk, as they say, outside any formal communication structure. It is even more flexible, as you may veer away from ritualistic conventions, and just be yourself – or not. The way you informally bond with your friends at work may be entirely different from how you converse with your siblings, as with your childhood best friends, and with your spouse.

Interacting formally and informally both employ the verbal and nonverbal elements of communication, using both words and non-words. In order to be an effective communicator, you have to be able to recognize when it is appropriate to be formal or otherwise, and how to maintain the protocol in case the former is required.

Chapter 3. Keys to an Effective Communication

Communication Arts is a course subject taken by scholars, and is also an entire program for those who would like to major in it. This, as it is proves that indeed, communication is an art. But why is it not as popular to take up a course with the title, Communication Skills?

There is some notion about describing something as an art, apart from being a skill, but the truth is that skills are part of what comprises an art. The word, art, is defined as 'something that is created with imagination and skill and that is beautiful or that expresses important ideas and feelings'. To create art requires skills, thus the art of communicating requires communication skills. What then are communication skills? What does it take to communicate effectively?

Perhaps one of the most important communication experiences you might have or might still face is being on a job interview. This is when you are expected to put your best (better) foot forward, so to speak, with the goal of getting the job. You are aware that it is in this kind of setting that your communication skills are most deliberately being gauged, as effectively communicating with superiors, colleagues and staff, is crucial in the success of any company.

However, whether you are communicating to obtain your most coveted job, to impress the partner of your dreams, or to revive a broken relationship, you should be able to make sure you convey exactly what you intend to, and you understand what they are trying to say, as well. This is effective communication. How can you do this?

The primary step

The prerequisite to any success is becoming aware of yourself, as much as possible. Have you ever caught yourself looking at others' failures, flaws and mistakes, as well as their successes, positivity and strengths? Well it's about time you focus on yours. How much are you familiar with your strengths and weaknesses? Have you even exerted effort to know?

To learn is to unlearn, and to unlearn is to be aware. In order for you to learn how to be effective in anything, you are required to know what you know and what you do not. What you already know may make or break you, and so does what you don't. What you already know may either be beneficial or not, and the fact that you are not as knowledgeable on something may be the same. What you already know may be either enhanced or changed, and only by your own will are you allowed to choose.

What should you know about yourself in as far as effective communication is concerned then? You may start by thinking about the worst experience you ever had while trying to converse with another person. Was it with a parent, a colleague, a superior or a junior? Was it in a face-to-face encounter or was it through an email? Where did the misunderstanding originate? What went wrong? By reflecting on the answers to these questions, you will be able to identify patterns upon which you weaknesses lie.

Once you have determined your weaknesses, it is time to look into possible remedies. It is time to unlearn these patterns and learn new strategies, which you may already add to the list of strengths you can identify by thinking of the most successful communication experiences you have had in different settings. As you assess yourself on these areas, ask yourself further:

Are you having difficulty in understanding the situation, the message or the other person?

Can you deliver the message accurately and concisely?

What is your level of convincing ability?

Are you able to actively listen, while being attentive and observant?

Do you find trouble in recognizing whether or not you were able to convey the message correctly?

Having the answers to the aforementioned questions in mind, you may want to know what it takes to improve communication skills. While some have managed to enumerate more and more 'communication skills' you have to learn, what follow are just two very basic things you have to keep in mind to become an effective communicator. First is listening, and the second one is keeping it clear, concise and coherent.

1. Genuine listening

Have you experienced being at your lowest, seeking for someone you can pour your frustrations to – someone you can trust, someone who won't judge. You call your friend, go on a coffee date, and cry your heart out, trying to exhaust whatever time will allow you to. Your friend, being ever-sympathetic, tells you all the reasons you should not be wasting your time on what you are going through, enumerates all the other more worthwhile things to spend your energy on, and says all those nice things you might want to hear. You become bombarded of what your companion keeps talking about, despite the sincerity and valuable efforts. You suddenly realize you could have just done it over the phone or probably in an email, so only you can do the talking – because you wanted an ear, not an amplifier. You were not looking for a shrink; you needed a listener.

Considering its role in the whole communication process, listening could be described as a skill comprising so many other skills. For you to be a genuinely good listener, you should be able to be sensitive, empathetic, sincere, and also, yes, appropriate. You should be able to juggle all these qualities in order for your listening ability to turn into a listening skill.

For your listening experience to be an embodiment of your sincerity, you need to be sensitive of the needs of the person you are conversing with. As such, your antenna should be armed with loads of empathy, or the ability to 'put your feet in the shoes of others'. Listen to both what they are and are not saying, being careful not to overdo it, as doing so puts the entire communication process at a risk of defeating its purpose. Remember that by being empathetic, you are able to allowed to enhance your sensitivity or ability to sense the very needs of the person you are conversing with, thus charging your sincerity, and enabling you to determine how to act appropriately – when to speak, when to not; when to maintain a distance, and when to touch.

Becoming a genuine listener requires the human being in you – that which rests beyond the realms of the technology behind whichever medium of communication there is.

2. Keeping it clear, concise and coherent

There are stylistic conventions in communications, be in oral or written. Although more usually employed in formal settings, these standards are also relevant in informal settings, as they stand not only as mere conventions, but also as means to make communication, regardless of type, more effective. These characteristics of an effective communication include clarity, conciseness and coherence.

Clarity

The quality of being easily understood, in a very exact way, is clarity. It is like looking onto the surface of a lake, and being able to see that the things at its bottom won't hurt you. This knowledge allows you therefore to step out of your boat and take a dip, because you know for sure that doing so will not put you in danger. There is no vagueness, no ambiguity, no generality.
A clear message hits the bull's eye. It is very specific, you will not be confused because of the vagueness of its construction nor of how it has been delivered. When you say, 'go get the bottle of water seated at the second layer of the fridge's shelf', the receiver will be more able to perform as you instructed rather than when he or she is told to 'just go get it there'.
If your message is constructed and delivered with clarity, you, its sender also avoid multiplicity of meanings. When you talk about a ruler, for instance, you may be interpreted as speaking about either a

device that is used to measure things, or a leader or a government. When you describe your boss as toxic, people may think you are saying he or she contains poisonous substances, when you actually mean that he or she gives you so much stress at work. In making your statements clear or free from ambiguity, you only need to contextualize, or provide information about the specific situation in which the subject of your talk or writing happens.

If you want to make your message clear it should be free from general statements. In this guideline, the difference between description and definition is significant. If you are asked to describe a snake and you say, 'an animal that crawls', you might be mistaken to be describing a worm. If you say, 'a scary creature', the word you are describing might be interpreted as a monster, or probably the receiver's mother-in-law. What you did in these two examples is describe a snake, while its clearer definition may be 'a limbless reptile that is usually venomous'.

Conciseness

'Keep it short and simple' is a common advice given to public speakers, as they would not want their audience to snooze or leave the hall during a talk. In business writing, correspondence is expected to be brief and direct, because readers of such have so much to do, they cannot afford to read unnecessary paragraphs when you are only requesting for a use of their hall. Even in casual conversations, you would not want your friends to get bored while you share the story of how you found new dog, neither would you want a prospective partner in life to get turned off because you 'talk too much'.

Conciseness is another characteristic of a good strategy to communicate well. It refers to the brevity of expression or statement, free from all unnecessary detail. This does not go to say that you have to limit your words, or miss out on the significant items. Brevity does not conclusively mean a little; moderation and necessity do the trick. Incorporating empathy and sensitivity through active listening, you may be able to determine when there is need for elaboration, and when the number of words you are using is exceeding the capacity of your receiver. So there again, moderation is key.

Coherence

What you say should be what you mean.
In order for you to make yourself comprehensible in a conversation, or in a chat room or inbox, master the property of being logical and well-organized in your words and actions so that you may be easily understood, and not mistaken to be saying something else. This can be done by using appropriate pauses, tone of voice, hand gestures, and other essential nonverbal signals to consistently back up what you actually want to convey. In written communication, it is important that you work on your structure by being careful with spelling and grammar, using the right, simple words, and not mixing too many ideas in one paragraph.
It also helps to make use of proper transitional devices. These are tools that give cohesion to your paragraphs and sentences. They are like bridges between parts of your paper, helping the reader to interpret ideas in the

way that you, as a writer, want them to understand. Examples of these are the following:

To show sequence: first, second, third; next, then, following this; simultaneously, concurrently...

To give an example: for example, for instance; in this case, in another case; to illustrate, in illustration...

To summarize or conclude: in brief, all in all, summing up; in conclusion, therefore...

Delivering your statements and responding in order makes you for victorious in getting the results you want. If your goal is to be understood, it is necessary to make yourself understood. Not everybody makes an effort to take an extra mile analysing what you really mean. Not everybody has the luxury of time to figure out your cultural background, your family history, your educational attainment, or your personality, just to make you successful in making yourself understood. While the persons you converse with indeed have a major role in the accomplishment of a communication process, you complete the other half of this 'major role'. Make sure you observe brevity and completeness alike when conversing verbally or in written form.

Whether spoken or in written, formal or informal, keeping an organized structure in communication is important in ensuring its effectiveness. Incorporating the necessities imbedded in genuine listening, keeping the clarity, conciseness and coherence of communication, while continuously staying self-aware, will indeed make you a better speaker or listener, and a better writer or reader.

Final Words

Generally, regardless of which setting you are in, you can be able to talk and connect with anyone by being yourself with confidence, while staying sensitive with whatever needs may arise from the situation so that you may be able to act accordingly.

Whether you are a sender or a receiver or a message, your involvement in the communication process is affected not only by your communication skills, but also by your attitude, your knowledge, your social system and your cultural upbringing. It is also worth remembering that aside from content, the message includes its elements, treatment, structure and codes, and that the channel, makes use of one's hearing, seeing, touching, tasting and feeling. In a continuous processes, in which you initially acted as a receiver, you may eventually take the role of the sender of a message to either the initial sender, or another person. The most important thing to remember is that the goal of the communication process, is to make it effective, that is, having the receiver understand precisely what the sender intended to convey.

As it goes, practice makes perfect. You can only improve if you do not stop doing it. Stay passionate about communicating with people who vary in all aspects — age, gender, race, cultural background, religious affiliations, political beliefs and socioeconomic status, among so many others. Have a conscious goal of improving at each deliberate attempt, until it becomes natural for you to express yourself appropriately from a one-on-one meeting, to a public speaking event.

Thank You Page

I want to personally thank you for reading my book. I hope you found information in this book useful and I would be very grateful if you could leave your honest review about this book. I certainly want to thank you in advance for doing this.

www.ingramcontent.com/pod-product-compliance
Lightning Source LLC
LaVergne TN
LVHW021746060526
838200LV00052B/3507